SCHIRMER'S LIBRARY
OF MUSICAL CLASSICS

Vol. 2047

ANTONIO VIVALDI

The Four Seasons

Four Concertos for Violin and Orchestra

COMPLETE
Spring
Summer
Autumn
Winter

For Violin and Piano Reduction

Violin part edited by Rok Klopčič
Piano reduction by Alojz Srebotnjak

ISBN 978-0-6340-7897-2

G. SCHIRMER, *Inc.*

DISTRIBUTED BY

7777 W. BLUEMOUND RD. P.O. BOX 13819 MILWAUKEE, WI 53213

FOREWORD

Around 1725, the Amsterdam publisher Michele Carol Le Cene published Vivaldi's series of twelve concertos for violin solo, strings and continuo under the title *Il Cimento dell' Armonia e dell' Inventione*. The first four concertos of this "Test of Harmony and Invention" are named for the four seasons.

Il cimento was dedicated to the Venceslao Conte di Marzin, and from the wording of the dedication it is evident that the *Four Seasons* had been known and played for some years. However, for that edition Le Cene added "marginal notes of descriptive character related to the events depicted by the music." The author of these sonnets is not mentioned, but it was probably the composer himself.

The violin part in the piano score is an exact reproduction of Vivaldi's original text as printed in the orchestral score published by Instituto italiano Antonio Vivaldi (artistic director Gian Francesco Malipiero) in 1950. The piano reduction is by Alojz Srebotnjak; the separate violin part is the present editor's version. Dynamic markings and other editorial suggestions have been placed in brackets.

R.K.

CONTENTS

———

PERFORMANCE NOTES

SPRING

1. The characteristic endings in measures 125, 146, and 183 are printed as given in the previously mentioned edition by Instituto italiano Antonio Vivaldi:

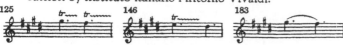

   However, some performers believe that all three endings should have the trill on the first note only (as originally written in measure 146)

2. In measure 197, the second D-sharp should perhaps be changed to D-natural.

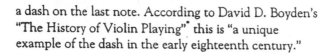

3. Throughout measures 170-179, the figure  was written by Vivaldi with

   a dash on the last note. According to David D. Boyden's "The History of Violin Playing"[*] this is "a unique example of the dash in the early eighteenth century."

SUMMER

1. In the first movement, measure 31, "e tutto sopra il canto" means "and all on the II. string". In measure 39 "sopra il cantino" means "on the I. string".

2. In the third movement, E-natural in measure 246 is original. All other E's in the same passage (mm. 244, 245 and 248) are given in the original as E-flat. This is probably a mistake of the composer or his copyist and all E's in this passage should be E-natural—as is generally played and printed in this edition.

3. In the third movement, mm. 247-250, the original part of the solo violin has "sopra il tenore e basso" i.e. on the III. and IV. strings. Many performers play these measures as "bariolage":

4. In this edition, measures 313 and 315 of the third movement give the second group as it is written in the original. Many violinists prefer this group to be played with two F-sharps:

AUTUMN

1. In the first movement, measure 89, of the original score, "e larghetto" was given only in the second violin part.

2. In the second movement, measure 4, "con sordino" is original.

3. In the second movement, measure 147, marking "p" is original.

WINTER

1. In the first movement, measure 4, Vivaldi specified the trill for the first four notes only. Usually these trills are played on all the notes until the end of measure 11 and—by analogy—in measure 19, and again in the measures 40 to 43.

2. In the first movement, measure 13, the trill is not original, but is suggested by analogy with the trills in measures 16 and 17 which are original.

---

[*] Oxford University Press, 1965.

Spring
from
THE FOUR SEASONS

Antonio Vivaldi (1676-1741)
RV269

All is gay, and the birds sing happily.

FLOWING FOUNTAINS
Fountains play in the breeze, constantly moving.

THUNDER
The skies are dark; lightning flashes and thunder roars.

SONG OF THE BIRDS

After the storm, the birds return with their song.

THE SLEEPING GOATHERD

On the flowered meadow, the goatherd and his dog roam among the blossoming trees.

PASTORAL DANCE

Nymphs and shepherds dance to the bagpipes under the beautiful skies of spring.

Summer

from
THE FOUR SEASONS

Antonio Vivaldi (1676-1741)
RV315

LANGUISHING IN THE HEAT

Man and beast wilt in the burning sun; even the evergreens feel the heat.

THE CUCKOO
The Cuckoo sings loudly

THE DOVE

And the songs

(Allegro non molto)

(Allegro non molto)

of the turtledove and goldfinch are ardent.

THE GOLDFINCH

The gentle breezes sigh,

CHANGING WINDS.
but the north wind suddenly appears

and starts to quarrel.

THE NORTH WIND

A frightened shepherd weeps in fear and bemoans his fate

The fierce lightning and terrible thunder makes the shepherd unable to rest his weary body

175 BLUE-BOTTLE FLIES

THUNDER

TEMPESTUOUS SUMMERTIME

The shepherd is right to be afraid. The sky flashes and the thunder is awesome. Grain and fruit are destroyed by the storm.

Autumn
from
THE FOUR SEASONS

Antonio Vivaldi (1676-1741)
RV293

The peasants dance and sing, hailing the fruits of the harvest.

The drunkard drinks deeply from the cup of Bacchus.

The Drunks

The drunkards fall into a deep slumber.

The drunkards sleep soundly; the season is mild; peace and rest overtake all the joyous peasants.

The Hunt

As dawn breaks the hunter appears with his horn, hound, and gun.

The prey appears; the chase in on.

The prey is bewildered by the clamorous dogs and the noise of the guns.

Fatigued and wounded, the prey falls and dies.

Winter

from
THE FOUR SEASONS

Antonio Vivaldi (1676-1741)
RV297

We run and stamp our feet at every step.

Our teeth chatter with the cold.

We pass the day contented by the fireside; outside it is raining very hard.

We slip and fall.

(falling down) 130

We get up and bravely try again.

170 The ice is breaking, the cracks are wide.

The sirocco wind howls around each bolted door.

The shrieking winds are at war.

Such is winter, but it has its joys.

Violin

SCHIRMER'S LIBRARY
OF MUSICAL CLASSICS

Vol. 2047

ANTONIO VIVALDI
The Four Seasons
Four Concertos for Violin and Orchestra

COMPLETE

For Violin and Piano Reduction

Violin part edited by Rok Klopčič
Piano reduction by Alojz Srebotnjak

ISBN 978-0-6340-7897-2

G. SCHIRMER, Inc.

DISTRIBUTED BY
HAL•LEONARD®
CORPORATION
7777 W. BLUEMOUND RD. P.O. BOX 13819 MILWAUKEE, WI 53213

Spring

from
THE FOUR SEASONS

Violin

Antonio Vivaldi (1676-1741)

RV269

Spring has returned.

SONG OF THE BIRDS

All is gay, and the birds sing happily.

FLOWING FOUNTAINS
Fountains play in the breeze, constantly moving.

THUNDER

45 The skies are dark; lightning flashes and thunder roars.

SONG OF THE BIRDS

After the storm, the birds return with their song.

VIOLIN

THE SLEEPING GOATHERD
On the flowered meadow, the goatherd and his dog roam among the blossoming trees.

PASTORAL DANCE
Nymphs and shepherds dance to the bagpipes under the beautiful skies of spring.

VIOLIN

Summer
from
THE FOUR SEASONS

Violin

Antonio Vivaldi (1676-1741)
RV315

LANGUISHING IN THE HEAT

Man and beast wilt in the burning sun; even the evergreens feel the heat.

THE CUCKOO

The Cuckoo sings loudly

VIOLIN

THE DOVE
And the songs of the turtledove

(Allegro non molto)

and goldfinch are ardent.

THE GOLDFINCH

The gentle breezes sigh,

CHANGING WINDS.
but the north wind suddenly appears and starts to quarrel.

THE NORTH WIND

A frightened shepherd weeps in fear

and bemoans his fate

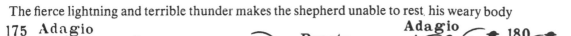

VIOLIN

The fierce lightning and terrible thunder makes the shepherd unable to rest, his weary body

TEMPESTUOUS SUMMERTIME
The shepherd is right to be afraid. The sky flashes and the thunder is awesome. Grain and fruit are destroyed by the storm.

This page has been intentionally left blank to facilitate page turns.

Autumn
from
THE FOUR SEASONS

Violin

Antonio Vivaldi (1676-1741)
RV293

The peasants dance and sing, hailing the fruits of the harvest.

The drunkard drinks deeply from the cup of Bacchus.

VIOLIN

The drunkards fall into a deep slumber.

The drunkards sleep soundly; the season is mild;
peace and rest overtake all the joyous peasants.

The Hunt
As dawn breaks the hunter appears with his horn, hound, and gun.

Allegro

The prey appears; the chase is on.

simile

The prey is bewildered by the clamorous dogs and the noise of the guns.

Fatigued and wounded the prey falls and dies.

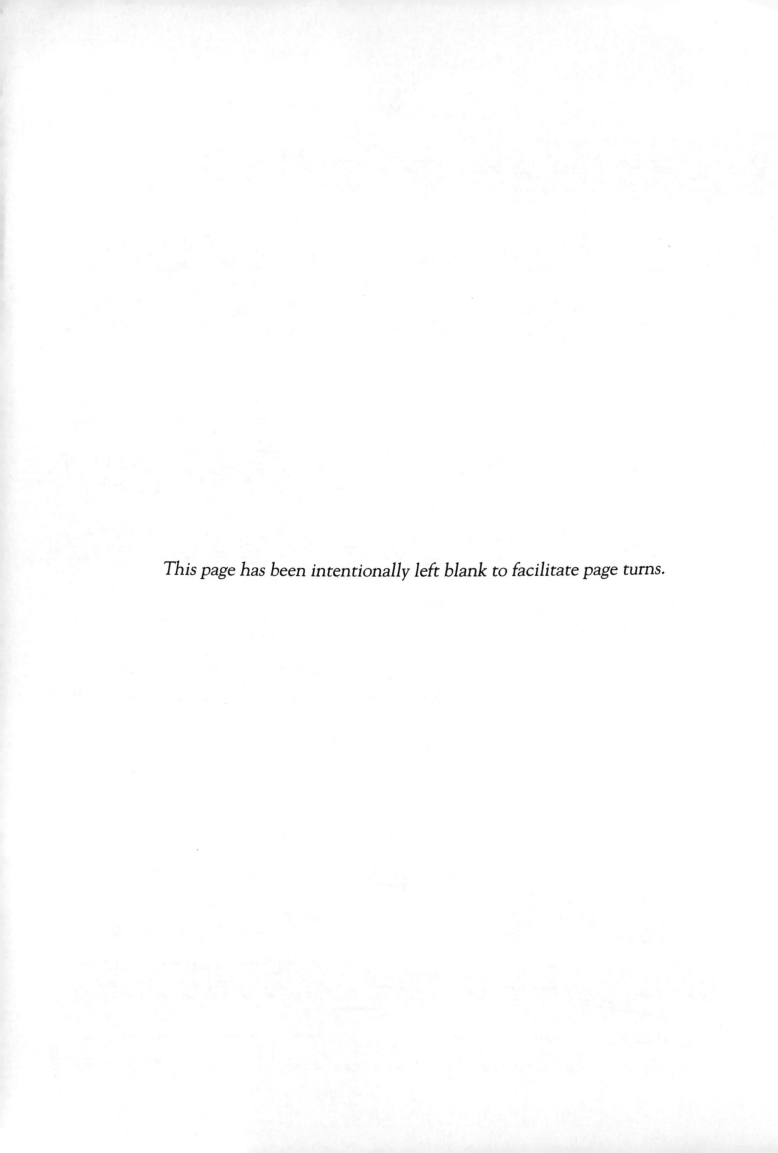

This page has been intentionally left blank to facilitate page turns.

Winter
from
THE FOUR SEASONS

Violin

Antonio Vivaldi (1676-1741)
RV297

We shiver in the snow
Allegro non molto

and are pierced by the cruel winds.

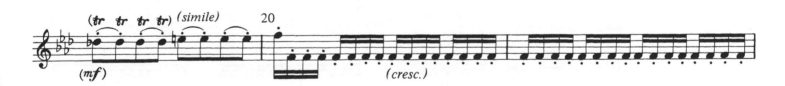

We run and stamp our feet at every step.

VIOLIN

Our teeth chatter with the cold.

VIOLIN

We pass the day contented by the fireside; outside it is raining very hard.

VIOLIN

The ice is breaking, the cracks are wide.

The sirocco wind howls around each bolted door.

Lento

The shrieking winds are at war.

Such is winter, but it has its joys.

PERFORMANCE NOTES

SPRING

1. The characteristic endings in measures 125, 146, and 183 are printed as given in the previously mentioned edition by Instituto italiano Antonio Vivaldi:

   However, some performers believe that all three endings should have the trill on the first note only (as originally written in measure 146)

2. In measure 197, the second D-sharp should perhaps be changed to D-natural.

3. Throughout measures 170-179, the figure was written by Vivaldi with

   a dash on the last note. According to David D. Boyden's "The History of Violin Playing"* this is "a unique example of the dash in the early eighteenth century."

SUMMER

1. In the first movement, measure 31, "e tutto sopra il canto" means "and all on the II. string". In measure 39 "sopra il cantino" means "on the I. string".

2. In the third movement, E-natural in measure 246 is original. All other E's in the same passage (mm. 244, 245 and 248) are given in the original as E-flat. This is probably a mistake of the composer or his copyist and all E's in this passage should be E-natural—as is generally played and printed in this edition.

3. In the third movement, mm. 247-250, the original part of the solo violin has "sopra il tenore e basso" i.e. on the III. and IV. strings. Many performers play these measures as "bariolage":

   etc.

4. In this edition, measures 313 and 315 of the third movement give the second group as it is written in the original. Many violinists prefer this group to be played with two F-sharps:

AUTUMN

1. In the first movement, measure 89, of the original score, "e larghetto" was given only in the second violin part.

2. In the second movement, measure 4, "con sordino" is original.

3. In the second movement, measure 147, marking "p" is original.

WINTER

1. In the first movement, measure 4, Vivaldi specified the trill for the first four notes only. Usually these trills are played on all the notes until the end of measure 11 and—by analogy—in measure 19, and again in the measures 40 to 43.

2. In the first movement, measure 13, the trill is not original, but is suggested by analogy with the trills in measures 16 and 17 which are original.

---

* Oxford University Press, 1965.